THE BUNGLED JUNGLE

By M. Anderson

Illustrated by Kelsie Constable

The lion in the jungle was a good and mighty king.
He wore a crown upon his head, he wore a golden ring.

He loved and cared for all the beasts
Who shared his jungle home;
They all would bow before him
Wherever he would roam.

But the king was growing old –
He removed his ring and crown –
“I’m too tired to rule,” he said.
“It’s time that I step down.”

So the lion packed his bags
And gave each beast a warm embrace.
He told them, “I am leaving now;
Someone must take my place.”

The animals grew worried –
They asked, “What shall we do?
We need to choose a leader,
That’s clearly true but WHO?”

"Pick one of us to be the king!"
Cried all the chimpanzees,
"So we're sure to have protection
For our homes up in the TREES."

"That settles it!" the chimps declared.
"This meeting is adjourned."

“But wait!” cried all the hippos,
“We’re still a bit concerned.”

We love to wallow in the mud;
We feel there is a need
To keep the RIVER flowing.”
(The elephants agreed)

Then swooping down into their midst,
There came a mighty bird.
He fanned his tail and strutted
And demanded to be heard.

"Trees and rivers are important,
But does anybody care
About the cranes who spend their days
Flying through the AIR?"

Then slithered in a python,
And he mentioned with a hiss,
"King or no king, this I know –
We can't go on like this!

Trees and rivers, air above –
All places beasts are found –
But I travel on my belly,
So save my home, the GROUND!"

Gorillas, zebras, and giraffes
Were voicing their concerns,
And mighty wildebeest begging
“Come now, wait your turns!”

They were speaking all at once,
And no one could be heard –
It was a bungled jungle
And it sounded quite absurd!

High above the hurly burly
Came a buzzing overhead;
It was a lowly poop fly –
Yes, POOP, that's what I said!

First he circled for a landing,
Then he settled on a stump;
He bumbled and he stumbled,
Then he landed on his rump.

A leopard tried to swat him,
Some baboons began to shriek –
The poop fly flapped his wings and cried,
"Please, just let me speak!

Pardon me for list'ning in –
I couldn't help but hear –
It seems we need a leader
For the home we all hold dear."

“Taking care of where we live
Is a proper thing to do,
And I would like to share with you
A different point of view.

Some want what is best for trees,
Some love the water more,
Some believe we need clean air,
Some love the jungle floor.”

“The jungle is our home,
But we aren’t being smart
If we only show concern
For just a single part.

Take a poop fly for example –
I work among the trees
To pollinate their blooms
With my friends, the helpful bees.

I also need the river –
Like you, it's where I drink –
To keep our water fresh and clean
Matters, don't you think?

I'm known to spend a lot of time
Flying high up in the air;
So like the birds, I'm interested
In how it looks up there.

But my favorite spot of all
Is right here on the ground,
For that is where the poop is
Where I like to hang around!"

When the poop fly mentioned poop,
The jungle beasts said...

EEEE

But they began to stop and think –
“What the poop fly says is true!”

The chimps all scratched their heads,
Then one dared to declare,
"Although we live in treetop homes,
We also need the air."

For when we swing from limb to limb,
The air is where we're at –
I guess you'd say the air
Is our part-time habitat!"

Then the creatures in the river said,
"It cannot be denied,
We all need the trees, as well,
For shade that they provide."

Then the warthog spoke his mind –
"I live down on the ground,
But when I need a bath," he said,
The river's where I'm found.

Votes

We need the ground and river
And the trees with sky above,
For these are all the parts
Of the jungle home we love!"

A voice cried out, "Let's hold a vote
So all can have a say
In what is best for all of us –
The democratic way!"

"Let's make a rule that from now on
We'll take better care of trees.
Together, we'll start planting!"
(That pleased the chimpanzees).

We'll put out the wildfires
To stop pollution in the air –
For fires fill the sky with smoke,
Let's keep it clean up there!

And we'll be careful with our river –
It needs protecting, too –
No building dams to stop it up,
But let it flow right through.

When we gather at the river,
We won't pollute the shore;
We'll leave no trace behind
Because we've never loved it more.

Next, the animals agreed,
"No matter where our homes are found,
We'll nevermore be careless
By throwing litter on the ground."

The creatures learned their lesson
About how every single part
Of the jungle is important
And dear to every heart.

They thanked their friend the poop fly
For he'd shown them all the key
To peaceful happy living
Which is how our lives should be.

They also thanked the poop fly
Who made them all aware
That voting is a way
To keep things fair and square.

“We like to vote,” they all declared, “For no one gets left out.
Democracy’s the way to go, we know without a doubt!”

Then all the jungle critters
Realized one more thing –
When they worked together,
They didn't need a king.

A king makes all decisions,
And nobody has a say;
Perhaps a president
Would find a better way.

When you have a president,
You vote for what you need –
"And we know voting works for us!"
The jungle beasts agreed.

A president's a leader
Who is picked by everyone.
They listen to the critters,
And they help them get stuff done.

“Let’s vote for our new president!”
The jungle beasts sang out.
Can you guess who they elected?
Poop fly, without a doubt!

VOTE

Made in the USA
Columbia, SC
17 August 2020